ROAD TO RECONCILIATION ...AND BEYOND

Unlikely Friends Become Brothers

Charles H. Norman III

ROAD TO RECONCILIATION...AND BEYOND
Unlikely Friends Become Brothers
Charles H. Norman III

Published November 2022
Heirloom Editions
Imprint of Jan-Carol Publishing, Inc.
All rights reserved
Graphic Design: Tara Sizemore
Cover Background Illustration: Maruba/Adobe Stock
Copyright © 2022 Charles H. Norman III

This book may not be reproduced in whole or part,
in any manner whatsoever, without written permission, with the
exception of brief quotations within book reviews or articles.
All photographs and permission of use provided by author.

ISBN: 978-1-954978-82-9
Library of Congress Control Number: 2022950117

You may contact the publisher:
Jan-Carol Publishing, Inc.
PO Box 701
Johnson City, TN 37605
publisher@jancarolpublishing.com
www.jancarolpublishing.com

Preface

What started out as an idea for an article for my monthly column in the *Glen Rose Reporter* newspaper (TX) evolved into something much bigger, much deeper, and much more personal than I ever could have imagined. Initially, I thought this would be an intriguing human-interest story about a 1960s singing group — made up of an eighth-grade English teacher and four students at his school — from my hometown of Odessa, Texas. However, it continued to grow into a story about this quintet *almost* making it really "big time" during the infancy of the "Doo-Wop" genre. Little did I know that Providence would have something much more significant, more touching, and more relevant.

I feel very privileged to have been given the opportunity to tell this true story about a teenage Black boy on the cusp of national music stardom. He experienced injustice, discrimination, and racism in the segregated society in which he grew up, but he overcame it all with love and forgiveness. My hope is to share this inspirational account with those who need acknowledgement that every person is equal in the eyes of God, along with those who need to have a better understanding of those with a different hue of skin, and that it would lead to a type of personal reconciliation and healing as well as for the eternal good. May you be blessed, entertained, and challenged as you read about what life was like in a country struggling to understand and live up to the Founding Fathers' decree that all men are created equal, endowed by our Creator with certain unalienable rights, including life, liberty, and the pursuit of happiness. May we all learn from the life Mark Prince lived.

Charles H. Norman III
ROAD TO RECONCILIATION...AND BEYOND
Unlikely Friends Become Brothers

Dedication

This book is dedicated to the memory of Pauline Branton Mack, my friend and initial contact person in preparing this story. She knew The Velvets during their schooldays, in the late 1950s and early 1960s, at Blackshear Junior/Senior High Schools. Pauline had been a personal family friend of mine for some 30 years and was the only person of color I knew from Odessa. A strong, devout Christian, Pauline was one of the sweetest, most caring individuals I'd ever known.

She grew up on the "Southside" of Odessa. Mr. Virgil Johnson was her junior high eighth-grade English teacher. Pauline was a fellow classmate of Mark, Clarence, Robert Earl, and William — the four guys who made up the "Doo-Wop" singers for Mr. Virgil and The Velvets. She loved them, and they loved her.

I contacted Pauline in an effort to reach Mark or Robert Earl, the last two surviving members of the group. She then put me in touch with Wanda Wallace Clayton, who provided me the necessary information to connect with Mark, who, at the time, lived in Fort Worth. (Robert Earl lives in Hawaii.) Though Pauline was in her last days and her health was swiftly deteriorating, Pauline knew I wanted to write a short story about The Velvets. And, through her efforts, I was able to meet Mark in late September of 2020.

Through labored breaths, Pauline talked to me on her phone in the ICU, saying, "Oh, Charles, I'm so happy. I'm so happy. You and Mark will be good for each other. You tell his story, for God has a story He wants told. You tell it, Charles. I'm so happy."

Shortly thereafter, I was meeting with Mark when we learned Pauline had had a heart attack. Mark and I joined in prayer for sweet Pauline, our mutual friend and initial common bond. Pauline never again regained consciousness. Eight days later, September 30, 2020, she entered God's Kingdom, where she is now happy forever and forever. It was exactly 13 years to the day that my dad had also entered the Kingdom. He was the man who first introduced me to sweet Pauline.

Though I was not able to give her a copy of this book – ROAD TO RECONCILIATION …AND BEYOND *Unlikely Friends Become Brothers* – I believe Pauline sees every line written from her dwelling place on high. So, this is that story.

Contents

Foreword	1
My Story	3
West Texas: The Story Begins	6
Road to Reconciliation …And Beyond	8
Time and Again	36
Virgil Johnson	38
Mark Prince	40
Clarence Rigsby	42
William "Solly" Solomon	43
Robert Earl Thursby	44
Sign of the Times	46
Mark Prince: Just a Regular Guy	52
Short and Sweet Meeting with Mark	54
Where Do We Go from Here	57
My Tribute to Mark Prince	60
And Beyond	63
About the Author	78
Acknowledgments	79

ROAD TO RECONCILIATION ...AND BEYOND

Unlikely Friends Become Brothers

Foreword

By Robert Earl Thursby
Last surviving member of The Velvets, 2022

Thank you, Charlie, for writing about The Velvets and meeting and developing a friendship with Mark Prince, my close friend and fellow singer. Since then, and because of Mark, we've also developed a friendship. I think it's great that you decided to focus on The Velvets, Blackshear High School, and what it was like growing up on the Southside back in our time. Your writing caused me to reminisce about growing up in Odessa, Texas, and the great times we had at Blackshear High School. I really miss those days and especially my times with Mark. We were very close. I remember graduation. I didn't really want to leave our school, but it was my time to go. I think it was very educational to grow up in Odessa, a very special place. Anyone who lived there for a length of time, I believe, would agree. Thank you again, Charlie, for writing ROAD TO RECONCILIATION …AND BEYOND. You captured a lot of what life was like on the Southside during those earlier years. Reading it brought back some very precious memories that were so much a part of my life. God bless you, my friend.

My Story

My earliest memory of being around a person of color is very faint. I seem to have a vague recollection of a nursemaid who helped my mom during the first couple of years of my life. It was a custom of that time, if people could afford it, to have a Black woman help a new mother tend to her newborn while adjusting to the new addition to the family. This was the way it was with my family. Perhaps the memory came from an old picture my parents took of me standing on the inside edge of my crib, and the Black lady standing nearby. I remember seeing the photograph many years ago. (I don't recall my folks ever using the N-word in a derogatory manner, but I do seem to remember them saying "negroes" and "coloreds" around the house.)

Seven or eight years later, when my grandfather developed Parkinson's disease, he needed some assistance getting around and taking care of himself. My dad and Aunt Nell hired a young Black fellow — he was in his late teens or early twenties — to stay with my granddad several hours each day. During this time (circa 1962), when I went to visit, I'd encounter this young helper. During one of our conversations, we started talking about sports and baseball, and he asked me if I knew how to throw a curve ball. I did not, so he proceeded to show me how to hold my fingers on the seam of the ball just so and how to flick my wrist a certain way as I threw the ball. Over time, I got to be pretty good at it, all thanks to that young Black fellow.

At that time, I was in the sixth grade and ran track for my school, the Fightin' Blue and Gold of Austin Elementary. My specialties were the 50-yard dash and the high jump. I was in Class F, the lightest class, which was for kids who weighed seventy pounds or less. One day, we had a track meet with a handful of other schools over on the "Southside," which was across the railroad tracks. I don't remember ever being over there before. There were also a bunch of Black kids from Douglass Elementary competing. I was too young and naïve to think much about the unfamiliar environment I found myself in or the competition I was facing. I was just there to run.

We lined up for the 50-yard dash. There were probably six of us in my heat, including a couple of Black kids. I ended up winning the race. Before I had time to savor my victory, though, one of those little Black boys came running up to me, wagging his finger in my face, saying, "I gonna beat you! Next time we run, I gonna beat you!" I was caught totally off guard. I just didn't understand.

A few weeks later, sure enough, we met again and had a rerun at the Odessa City-Wide Track Meet at Barrett Stadium. This time, there were over 20 schools competing for various class championships. My first event was the 50-yard dash. My Southside nemesis and four other boys were ready for the race. I felt a little tight. I guess he'd intimidated me alright, because he "smoked me" and everybody else.

Later that afternoon, I had loosened up and was much more prepared for the high-jump event. As I was getting ready to jump, I noticed my dad rolling my frail grandfather, who was in his wheelchair, out onto the field around thirty feet away from where I was about to jump. I think their presence and support gave me that little extra boost, and I won the event with a jump of four feet high. That win helped my school claim its first team trophy in decades. I was so proud of my team and school, the Fightin' Blue and Gold of Austin Elementary.

I don't recall ever carrying on a real conversation with a person of color until I was in college. That was my loss.

West Texas:
The Story Begins

As a young, Black teenager from West Texas, Mark Prince was on the cusp of national music stardom in 1960. He, three of his fellow classmates, and an eighth-grade English teacher at Blackshear, Mr. Virgil Johnson, formed one of the first-ever Doo-Wop singing groups of the era. With the help of their mentor, up-and-coming music star and fellow Texan Roy Orbison, The Velvets emerged as recording stars in their own right. But their hometown of Odessa hardly acknowledged or recognized their talent or the beautiful, harmonious sounds emanating from the Southside, right across the railroad tracks.

An oilfield boomtown of about around 80,000 residents at the time, Odessa was much like most cities in the South — segregated and content for the majority of its citizenry. With the city being approximately 95 percent White, it was more convenient to just let Black people live their own lives over on their side of town. As long as they didn't "stir the pot," that is. Because of necessity, for curiosity's sake, or for light mischievousness, sometimes Black people would venture across the tracks to get a glimpse of a different way of living. There, they could witness a higher standard of living, more opportunities to move up in life, and just see the way White folks lived their lives.

Mark and his friends sometimes journeyed across the tracks, and when they did, they would often times experience the sting of racism and prejudice.

It hurt. But because of Mark's upbringing — he was raised by loving, forgiving parents — and his faith, based on biblical truths taught to him by his church, he not only survived the social injustices and inequities he faced, but also he went on to have a successful career and life after the music dream died. Mark had a firm foundation and learned early on to exchange bigotry with love, bitterness with forgiveness, and denial with acceptance. What was true 60 years ago still rings true today. Our nation, and even our world, would be a better, more peaceful, more habitable place if we, as fellow citizens of this Earth, were to follow Mark's example.

> *"...But the greatest of these is love..."*
> 1 Corinthians 13:13, NIV

Road to Reconciliation ...And Beyond

Unlikely Friends Become Brothers

In the fall of 2020, while I was taking my regular walk around the soccer field park in Glen Rose, I was listening to *The Pat Boone Hour* oldies show on SiriusXM. I was stopped in my tracks by Pat, when he said something like this:

"Folks, now I'm going to play a genuine oldie from 1961...from one of the first-ever Doo-Wop singing groups. This group of five guys consisted of 25-year-old, junior high school English teacher Mr. Virgil Johnson and four students from his school, who served as his 'Doo-Woppers.' They were collectively known as The Velvets, and they all hail from the West Texas town of Odessa. I'll bet you'll recognize their biggest hit, their signature song from 1961, 'Tonight (Could Be the Night).' Ladies and gentlemen, The Velvets."

I vaguely remembered hearing that song, but had no idea those guys were from my hometown of Odessa! They were a little before my time, as I was only eleven in 1961. I know a lot about Odessa, but I knew nothing of The Velvets. I listened intently as the song played and instantly became a fan. The sound was so clean, clear, exuberant, and innocent, and there were such tight harmonies. I decided that when I got home, I would "Google" the group The Velvets and find out all I could. I became fascinated with their story.

l-r back: William Solomon, Clarence Rigsby, Robert Thursby; front: Mark Prince, Virgil Johnson

These guys were all from Blackshear Junior and Senior High School, on the Southside, an all-Black school that no longer exits. (Railroad tracks had divided the rest of Odessa from the Black community for decades. When integration came in the late '60s, Blackshear was eventually turned into a magnet elementary school.) The group was discovered by up-and-coming local recording artist and fellow West Texan Roy Orbison, and they signed a contract with Monument Records in Nashville. Within a three-year period, they had recorded some 30 songs. Along with Mr. Virgil's own composition, "Tonight (Could Be the Night)," their first song, called "That Lucky Old Sun," made the US charts. Another song "Lana," co-written by Roy Orbison and Joe Melson, even became a #1 hit in Japan in August 1961. As fate would have it, though, The Velvets slowly faded into musical history, and their recordings became a staple of the Doo-Wop genre and a bygone era.

After my initial research, I just had to know more. My first step was ordering their CD called *The Complete Velvets*. I loved it! I began delving deeper into the details of their story. I knew only one person of color in Odessa. Her name was Pauline, and she'd been a sweet family friend since the 1980s. Knowing she'd gone to Blackshear Junior and Senior High Schools around the time of The Velvets' formation, I called her up and asked if she happened to know any of those guys.

In her endearing, distinctive way, she said, "Land's sake, Charles. I knew all the boys. They were my classmates. Now, Mr. Virgil, he was my teacher! Everybody just loved Mr. Virgil."

Pauline told me — though I already knew because of Wikipedia — that only two of the quintet were still around. She thought that Robert Earl ("Bobby") lived in Hawaii and that Mark was maybe somewhere in the Dallas area.

I said to Pauline, "Boy, I sure would love to meet Mark if he'd be willing to talk with me. Think you might be able to contact him for me? And if so, tell him I'd love to write a story for my local newspaper, *The Glen Rose Reporter*."

Pauline loved the idea. Though her health was failing, 78-year-old Pauline told me she'd try to find his number. A couple of days later, through a contact Pauline gave me, I got Mark's phone number and was told he lived in Ft. Worth. He was only one hour from me! I asked my new contact, Wanda, if she'd be my go-between. She knew Mark personally through her work helping organize Blackshear reunions in Odessa. I wanted her to pave the way for me and reassure him of my honorable intentions. Wanda said that she would do that, and she did.

I called Mark and said, "Hi, Mark. I know you don't know me, but my name is Charlie. And I am a big fan of yours. I'm 70 years old, and I'm also from Odessa... from *way* back. I got your number through my dear friend and your former classmate, Pauline, and Wanda, the Blackshear reunion organizer in Odessa. I now live about an hour away from you, right down in Glen Rose."

I told Mark that I would love to know more about The Velvets' story and maybe even write about it. He replied with the words I was hoping to hear: "You come on, man. Come on! We'll talk!"

A few days later, I ventured to north Ft. Worth to begin a friendship that I was already sensing would do us both good. Mark was 78 years old, lived in a modest apartment by himself, and had arthritis, diabetes, and kidney and blood pressure issues. As a result, he didn't get around much. He cooked for himself and used a walker. He didn't drive, but he did have a younger sister and niece in the area who looked after him.

For over two hours, Mark and I got acquainted and became quite comfortable with each other. Mark shared so many memories.

I just had to ask, "How is it that you became a local star on the Southside at such a young age? What was that like?"

Mark proceeded to tell me his story, and this is it:

Back in November of 1959, while in his English class at Blackshear Junior High, his teacher Mr. Virgil Johnson said he'd heard "rumors" and wanted to know if any of the boys in class could sing. Mark immediately popped up and said, "I do! Me and Clarence do duets."

Mr. Virgil called them up to the front of the class and said, "Well, boys, let me hear whatcha got."

Mark had a low bass voice, and Clarence had a higher tenor voice. They hopped up, ready to shine, and did their thing. Mr. Virgil was blown away, as their fellow classmates applauded wildly. Mark and Clarence had been honing their harmonies for years while on their way to and from out-of-town ball games in the back of the Blackshear Band bus.

Virgil Johnson

An experienced singer in his own right, Virgil had sung in church choirs while growing up in Lubbock, Texas. While attending Bishop College in East Texas, he also sang with a group of fellow students who called themselves "The Dynatones." Shortly after taking the job at Blackshear in 1958, Mr. Virgil had the idea of possibly getting a group together to do some singing at sock hops, concerts, and talent shows in the community. He only wanted clean cut non-smokers and non-drinkers. He asked Mark if he knew any other boys who could sing and would maybe want to join a group.

Mark said, "I sure do."

Mark sang bass, Clarence sang tenor, Bobby and William "Solly" soon joined right in there. These young teens and Mr. Virgil, who possessed a strong, multi-octave lead tenor voice, became quite the polished singing quintet. They initially called themselves "The Veldaires," but later changed their name to The Velvets.

The group got permission from Principal E.K. Downing to use the auditorium for after-school practices and rehearsals. Because of the boys' natural singing talent, and the leadership of Mr. Virgil, they had something really

Mark Prince

Clarence Rigbsy

Robert Earl Thursby

William "Solly" Solomon

special. They worked very hard to develop the right dance moves to go along with each song. Though everyone in the group contributed, it was Clarence who was particularly good at coming up with perfectly coordinated routines that fit smoothly with their act. The precise, in-sync footwork and arm motions took a lot of practice, but they got it. The Velvets had the "it" factor before folks even knew what "it" was.

Principal E.K. Downing

The boys' parents, Mr. Virgil, and Mr. Walter Hunt (the Blackshear band director) all chipped in to help the group acquire spiffy, new matching outfits to wear at their performances. They wore Black tuxedos and bow ties for formal occasions, and they wore gray coats, white shirts, and matching maroon pants and ties for less formal appearances. Soon, the guys were singing at school dances and parties, performing at concerts, and performing at various Blackshear school events.

Mark told me that through The Velvets, he and the boys became "pretty popular with the little ladies." He said, "We'd all go to The Blue Front on the weekends. That was the local teen club where all the young people of color went to dance and flirt. Let's just say we fellas had no trouble finding dance partners. Who says you gotta be a football hero to get along with a beautiful girl? And let me tell you about The Blue Front. Miss Essie ran that place and ran it right, too. She made it clear that 'no bad words' or any type of shenanigans were allowed in her place. No, sir. Her son Arthur Ray was one big dude and served as a bouncer of sorts. So, let me just say, there was no mischief or horseplay at The Blue Front with Miss Essie

The Blue Front (2021)

and Arthur Ray around. It was a safe haven for dancing and clean fun. And, man, did we have fun!"

The Velvets were so good that they were soon able to venture out to a few other venues on the other side of town across the tracks. They were even special guests at the Lions Club luncheon at The Sands Restaurant, right on the fringe of the Southside in early 1961. The Velvets once had a concert right down the road, a couple of miles west of Blackshear, at Ector High School. This school was for White and Hispanic students who lived south of the railroad tracks.

One fellow named Don, who graduated from Ector High in 1962 and now lives outside Oklahoma City, remembered it well. He said, "Yeah, we actually rearranged our relatively large library for The Velvets. We moved all the chairs and tables to the sides of the room, and they set up at one end. I remember thinking, 'This is really strange,' because I'd never seen any Black people at our school before. Then the music and dancing began, and how great it was! I'll never forget their rendition of 'Duke of Earl.' It was that good, and that was 60 years ago! Man, were they good."

On occasion, The Velvets were even invited to perform and have concerts at the hoity-toity Odessa Country Club, where patrons would sometimes toss rolled up $100 bills at their feet to show appreciation for their talent. However, after performances, The Velvets duly retreated to their own community back on the Southside.

Because of The Velvets' obvious talent and infectious, friendly aura, they were occasionally invited to sing on the local TV station KOSA's live

show called *The Pioneer Furniture Jamboree*, which featured various local bands and artists on Saturday afternoons. Roy Orbison – who was regularly a guest artist on the show and who was riding high after his own first hit, "Only the Lonely" – also lived in the area and had been singing in and around the Odessa area for a few years. Roy was so impressed by the guys that he called Mr. Virgil and told him they should meet his record producer, Mr. Fred Foster, who had an up-and-coming company called Monument Records in Nashville. He was looking to sign a Black vocal group to his label.

Mr. Virgil sent a few song demos to Fred, and shortly thereafter Fred called Virgil and invited him and the boys to come to Nashville and do some recording at the renowned RCA Studio. The five of them, including the 25-year-old English teacher and the four mid-teenage lads from

Blackshear Jr./Sr. High, all piled into Mr. Virgil's Black '59 Corvair and headed for Music City, USA. It was the real "big-time!"

Mark said to me, "Can you imagine our excitement? We're off to Nashville, Tennessee, boys! A thousand miles away! Shoot, we could hardly go a mile across the railroad tracks in Odessa without causing suspicion… and there we were, on our way to Tennessee! Hallelujah!"

During their trip, the Corvair broke down in Little Rock, but Mr. Foster knew people, and arranged for their car to be repaired overnight, and the guys were back on the road to Nashville. They even got to stay at the historic El Dorado hotel, the place where many famous Black people, such as Martin Luther King, Jr., Harry Belafonte, and The Temptations had stayed when in Nashville.

The Velvets met with Fred Foster, and they were two songs into their audition when he stopped them cold. Mr. Foster signed them to a recording contract right then and there… on the spot! It was hard for them to comprehend what their mentor, Roy Orbison, had just fostered for them.

The Velvets were welcomed and accepted with open arms by the session musicians and the music community as a whole. Glen Campbell

Crowd Attracted To Talent Show

The largest crowd in the history of Blackshear High School filled the seats and stood in the aisles last night to watch the first annual talent show staged by teachers of Douglas, Carver and Blackshear schools in the Blackshear Gymnasium.

"The Charleston," presented by Mrs. J. J. Walker, Mrs. Arlene Robinson and Mrs. J. R. Downing, with L. Breedlove doing a comic part, was a headliner.

Three songs by L. S. Jackson, a Midland teacher guest, also were a feature. A guest number, "30-Second Lover," by the Veldaires was acclaimed. Virgil Johnson, a teacher, and four students, Mark Prince, Clarence Rigsby, Robert Thursby and William Soloman made up the quintet of singers.

Mrs. Loretha Williams and Walter L. Hunt sang a duet, "Danny Boy," and Lonia Rogers and Mrs. Dixie Washington also were applauded for their duet, "Trees."

February 26, 1959

Jazz Festival Planned Here

The first annual Jazz Festival planned at Blackshear High School as a yearly event, will be given at 8 p.m. Thursday in the Blackshear Auditorium. Admission will be 50 cents for students and 75 cents for adults the night of the show.

Advance tickets will cost 35 cents for students and 50 cents for adults.

The jazz festival is sponsored by the John H. Johnson Chapter of Quill and Scroll, national honor society for high school journalists.

The Swingin' Verdicts, a Blackshear High boys quintet; The Hearts, a boys and girls quintet; The Continentals, a male sextet; the Blackshear Stage Band, and The Velvets, who have been making hit records, will be on the program.

Blues, mood songs, popular ballads, and swing numbers are included in the program.

The Blackshear Stage Band, directed by Walter Hunt, will play "Rock and Reel," "Route 66," "Blue Moon" featuring Martha "Time and Again," by Odessa's hit songwriter, Roy Orbison is among numbers of the Velvets. Harmonica solos by Georg Claude Johnson will be a feature of the Continentals songs.

"Whispering Wind" is a popular number in the group to be presented by the Swinging' Verdicts.

May 7, 1961

Jazz Festival Scheduled Here

The first annual Jazz Festival at Blackshear High School will be held at 8 p.m. Thursday in the Blackshear Auditorium, with various singing groups and the Blackshear Stage Band appearing.

Admission at the door will be 75 cents for adults and 50 cents for students.

The sensational Velvets, a Blackshear quintet, who have recently completed their second Monument record, "Tonight Could Be the Night We Fall in Love," will be on the program.

"Tonight" has sold 34,000 discs in two weeks and is apparently headed for success equal to the Velvets' first record, "Lucky Old Sun." Billboard lists "Tonight" as a hit. Cashbox, which was out Wednesday, said, "The Velvets who broke into the top 100 with their 'Lucky Old Sun' should head straight back there with 'Tonight.'"

"Tonight" was written by Vergil Johnson, Blackshear High School teacher, who is leader of the quintet. Other singers are Mark Prince, Robert Thursby, Clarence Rigsby and William Solomon.

May 10, 1961

Benefit Events Are Scheduled

More benefit events to help in the campaign to start a Carter Woodson branch of the Odessa Boys Club were announced today as the half-way mark was reached in the drive for $6,000.

A talent show featuring "The Velvets," is scheduled at 8 p.m. Friday in the Blackshear High School Auditorium. Admission will be $1 for adults and 50 cents for students.

A basketball game is slated at 7:30 p.m. Monday in the Blackshear gymnasium, with the Harlem Stars playing the King's Pennywise Team, 1961 city league champions here. Bold Buie, famous one-arm basketball star of the Harlem Globetrotters, will be playing with the Harlem Stars. Admission will be $1.25 for adults and 75 cents for students. Half of the gate receipts will go to the boys club fund.

May 7, 1961

Recording Group To Give Program

The Velvets, a group of five Odessa singers, who recently won a four-star rating from Billboard with a new hi-fi record, will present a program at the Wednesday noon meeting of the Tri-Service Lions Club in the Sands Restaurant.

The singers are Mark Prince and William Solomon, both seniors at Blackshear high School, Robert Thursday and Clarence Rigsby, students at Blackshear last year, and Virgil Johnson, English instructor at Blackshear.

February 28, 1961

The Odessa American (Odessa, Texas)

and The Everly Brothers befriended them. Anita Kerr of the renowned "Anita Kerr Singers" invited them all over to her house, where she sat at her piano and listened closely as they sang their repertoire of songs for her. She scribbled notes on her music sheets for each song, and the next day the string arrangements were all ready for them to use in their recordings.

Once, when The Velvets were in the studio recording, Anita approached Mark (who was 5'7" and weighed a whopping 127 pounds on a good day) and said to him, "Pound for pound, Mark, you've got the smoothest bass voice I've ever heard." What a compliment for a young Black boy who'd never set foot outside the state of Texas!

Boots Randolph played saxophone for the sessions, and Floyd Kramer added his magic touch on piano. Bob Moore played bass, and guitarists Hank Garland and Harold Bradley lent their sublime talents to each recording as well. These were top-notch professionals in these sessions, and because The Velvets knew their songs so well, it usually only took two or three takes, and they were done.

Mark told me that his favorite song they ever recorded was their version of "Crying in the Chapel." He just loved their unique, faster-paced, upbeat cover of one of Elvis's greatest hits. It was a whole new world for these talented young Odessans. And they loved it.

Mark also said, "Musicians don't see color." This was so refreshing and enlightening for the young singers to experience.

While on one of their three trips to Nashville to record, they attended an Ike and Tina Turner concert and were even invited to join the duo and their band on stage to perform.

In the spring of 1961, The Velvets' song "Tonight (Could Be the Night)," an original composition by Mr. Virgil, made it to #12 on one of the US pop charts. They became known nationwide as one of the very first original Doo-Wop groups of the genre.

But like most of the country at the time (especially the South), Odessa was segregated, and Jim Crow laws were the rule. When The Velvets performed on the other side of the tracks, they pretty much sang their songs, entertained their audience, and then scooted on back across to the Southside, Blackshear, and The Blue Front.

I asked Mark what it was like hearing their songs on the radio for the first time. He said, "It was the greatest feeling I've ever had. I'll never, ever forget it."

Though they had offers to tour the country, and even an invitation to do a stint in Las Vegas, and as great as all that was, Mr. Virgil felt his true calling was to continue on as an educator. He had family responsibilities at home, and the boys were still in school. Because of all of this – along with The Velvets' aversion to air travel – touring and promoting their records (which would be necessary to maintain momentum) were just not practical. So, the group mainly just performed in the Black community and recorded a few more songs that never charted.

Most Odessans never even heard about The Velvets. They might have heard their songs on the radio (most likely on KOSA), but few people knew the singing group resided just across the tracks on the other side of town. Local media coverage was minimal, and even that was only announcement-type publicity.

One fellow English teacher who taught in the Ector County School District for decades — now in her late 80s and living in Austin, Texas — worked with Mr. Virgil Johnson on the district's textbook committee and other curriculum-related projects. She told me that she never even knew Mr. Virgil was a recording artist, much less the lead singer of a group with a hit record on the national charts. She just knew him as the well-respected, well-dressed quality educator that he was. That was just the way it was back then — a sad sign of the times. Odessa missed out.

The Velvets disbanded when Mr. Virgil accepted a new job as principal of Dunbar-Struggs Junior High School in his hometown of Lubbock.

Earlier, in the write-up included with their CD song compilation (THE COMPLETE VELVETS Ace Records, 1996), Mr. Virgil explained that the group was extremely popular with Whites but was never extremely popular with Blacks. He explained, "We were Black, but we didn't sound like it. People didn't know we were a Black group except, of course, in Odessa. We couldn't tour, and that really hurt us."

The breakup nearly killed Mark, because as long as he could remember, even as a kid, all he'd wanted to do in life was sing. He grew up listening to his daddy's Count Basie and Duke Ellington records. Mark would sing along, feel the beat, and let the music become a part of him. He grew up singing in the church choir at Carter Chapel Church (CME), which was on the corner of Dixie and Murphy on the Southside. Occasionally, he would sing solos for the small congregation, all the while not knowing he was actually preparing himself for the bigger things that were soon to come. Mark also listened intently to Reverent Terrell's sermons about loving and forgiving those who mistreat

Carter Chapel Church

you, and that, too, became a part of who Mark was. Whenever there were opportunities at family gatherings and other events, Mark wanted to entertain, and he did. He was a natural. It haunted him the rest of his days that The Velvets almost made it "big-time" but didn't.

When Mark and I discussed his story, we opened up to one another in a way I'd never expected or experienced before. I felt led to really "go there" in terms of asking about race and discrimination, and because I had gained Mark's trust, he was willing. What could have been a little awkward, Mark made easy. Because we had become friends who accepted each other no matter what, he allowed me to probe.

"Let's talk Odessa and what it was like growing up there as a Black kid in the late '50s, early '60s," I said to Mark.

"Okay, let's do it, Charlie," Mark replied.

"Mark, I know you had your own community over there on Southside," I said.

"Well, that's right. We had community. Everybody knew everybody. Most of the time we just stayed on our side of town. I mean, we had pretty much all we needed — schools, teams, bands and choirs, grocery stores, cleaners, churches, eatin' places, ball fields, skatin' rink, hangouts... even our own teenage dancing spot, The Blue Front, the one I told you about. You name it. Maybe not the variety or kind of quality you might find on the other side, but we made do. Many in the Black community had jobs over there and would drive over or commute to work on the bus, but our lives were really on the Southside." Mark explained.

"Did you have a doctor or access to medical care in your community?" I asked.

"Oh yeah, we Blacks had our own doctor there – Dr. Wheatley Stewart. Such a good, kind compassionate man. He had a little clinic over on Murphy Street, and his wife worked with him as a nurse. Sometimes we folks didn't have enough money to pay for his services, but he'd treat'em anyway and told them they could just pay later or bring him some of their homegrown vegetables, fruits, or eggs. Often times, Dr. Stewart would just say, 'We'll get it next time.' Now, when it was a big-time emergency, he'd accompany his patient to the big regional hospital across the tracks, where they'd allow him to treat his patients and perform surgery, if necessary. But *that* would have to be in the basement of the hospital." (Decades later, Dr. Stewart was honored by the city of Odessa and Odessa Regional Medical Center by them naming a wing of the area hospital after him – the Dr. Wheatley Stewart Medical Pavillon.)

"Mark, when you did venture across the tracks, what did you do or like to do?" I asked.

"Well, we did have freedom to go over there alright, you see, but we also knew things. And we knew there were places where there were restrictions for us Black folks. Sometimes we'd be called the "N-word" or worse or looked at suspiciously if we happened to be in an area where they weren't used to seeing people of color. Some places we had free access, but some others, not so much... like the roller-skating rink in town. During my growin' up time, we just knew that was a place we weren't really welcomed. Now, of course, that changed later, and that was good. But, you know what, we had our rink for us kids on the Southside. Small and dusty alright, but it was ours, and we still had our fun."

"The Rink"

"Boy, Mark, I was just too young to know about this stuff," I said.

"Yeah, I know," Mark said. "There were also the public buses, which many Black folks were compelled to use to get to work on the other side of town. Most of us didn't have money for a car. We knew our place on the bus… it was *Blacks* in the back."

"Really? What would happen if you tried sitting up closer to the driver?" I asked.

"Well, depending on the driver, sometimes we'd just sit there, and sit there, and sit there, the bus not moving… until *we moved* to our 'proper place' in the back. Then, the bus would start rolling again, as if nothing happened," Mark replied.

"Man, I had no idea. I was just naïve and ignorant, I guess. I'm so sorry," I said.

"Charlie, no need to apologize. That wasn't you. It was just a sign of the times."

"Well, okay then, what about those really nice clothiers downtown? Could you shop there?" I asked.

"Once again, Charlie, depends. For example, in the very early '60s, there were two or three pretty upscale clothing stores there, and for at least one of them… let's just say they 'strongly discouraged' us from coming in to browse and shop. Of course, most of us didn't have much money anyway, and probably couldn't afford anything they were selling. But we knew they didn't want us in there. I think the owners of these establishments felt like a lot of places in Odessa… that if they allowed people of color in a particular place, it might chase off the Whites who wouldn't want to patronize a business that allowed Blacks in," Mark explained.

I was taken aback hearing these things. "Gee, Mark, how'd you handle all that stuff?" I asked.

"Charlie, like I said, I know that wasn't you or people like you. My parents taught me and my sister to just let it go. Don't allow bitterness to seep in. Gotta forgive. Gotta forgive. No room in my heart for hate. And in time, things did change for the better," Mark said.

"This is so commendable of you, my friend. Boy, am I learning things! What about your teachers in school? Did you have any favorites?" I asked.

"Sure did," Mark said. "We had great teachers, Charlie. Our band instructor, Mr. Hunt and his wife... I'll never forget how kind and caring and generous they were to us kids. Then there was Mrs. Downing, the principal's wife and my seventh grade English teacher. She instilled in me the love of reading and history and that's stayed with me all my days."

"Any others?" I asked.

Miss Whitiker

"Yes, sir. Miss Whitiker. Miss Frizella Whitiker. Anybody and everybody who went through Blackshear had Miss Whitiker for junior and senior English. First word that comes to mind about Miss Whitiker — *disciplinarian*. She was strict, tough, and made us tow the line. But you know, Charlie, we knew she loved us. She had a way of sharing with us kids the knowledge, the wisdom, and smarts in her mind and put it in ours. She knew what we'd be facing in the future and was always trying to prepare us for that day. Man, sometimes we kids would be horse playing or cuttin' up in the hall, and then out of nowhere we'd find ourselves being dragged by our ear to the principal's office. It hurt too. No wonder my left ear sticks out a little bit more than it should. Ha! Sometimes, again out of the blue, she'd catch one of us kids from behind right at the collarbone and neck and get to pinching as she marched us off to our fate, to face our principal, Mr. Downing. Man, did she have a strong set of pinching fingers. Lots of practice, I guess. All that said, and though we were sorta scared of her, we knew she cared for us."

Mark continued, "Gotta tell you one fun story about me, the boys, and Miss Whitiker. Never forgot it either. Here we were, probably ninth or tenth

Mural on the Southside, featuring Doc Bracy's half weenie hotdog!

graders, taking our bathroom break. One of us had a cigarette, and we lit that thing up in the bathroom, and each of us started taking a puff and passing it on to the next boy. There was probably four or five of us just puffin' away, having a good ol' time, acting all tough and grown up. All of a sudden, that bathroom door burst open, and it was Miss Whitiker hollering, 'What you boys doin' in here?!' We almost wet our pants. She musta had a keen sense of smell, for she knew *exactly* what we were doing. Man, man. I tried to get rid of that cigarette, and all I could think of was to shove it in the urinal. And that's what I did. The evidence was still evident. Ugh! I can laugh at all that now, but it was definitely no laughing matter back then. No, sir, not with Miss Whitiker roaming the halls. The word at Blackshear was, 'No messin' where you shouldn't be a messin' when Miss Whitiker's around.' How I appreciate and love that Miss Whitiker." (Even today, the 93-year-old Miss Whitiker is the well-respected matriarch of the Black community and still lives in Odessa.)

"Wow, Mark, what fun stories!"

I then asked about the picture shows in town. "Can we talk about the movie theaters in town? Could you go there?"

"Well, pretty much... especially the smaller, cheaper ones. Now, the nicer ones in town actually had separate restrooms and drinking fountains for the

Whites and the Blacks, as well as a seating section in the balcony for Blacks only. That was okay. Some of us didn't go there, though. I'm told (ha!) many times Blacks would get a cheap bag of popcorn and flick kernels over the railing to pester the White kids below. We'd act all innocent-like and engaged in the movie whenever an usher was spotted making his way up the stairs to try to catch us, *er, uh, them,* in the act. And all that did change when the 1964 Civil Rights Act came around, and we had access to go anywhere we pleased. Like I said, that's just the way it was for a lot of places back then," Mark said.

Mark continued, "We liked to go to the drive-ins too, mainly the Cactus or the Broncho. Didn't matter. Sometimes two of us, sometimes there'd be six of us. If there was six of us, there'd be two in the front seat and four of us crammed in the trunk. Our driver would pay the two-dollar entry fee, go through the gate, find the best parking spot, pop the trunk, and the four of us would scramble outta there like bees in a beehive and into the car… three in the front and three in the back. Now, that was fun! So, guess what? For those two dollars we all enjoyed the show… let's see… that averages to about thirty-five cents a person for a two-hour movie. Not bad, huh?"

"And man, howdy, we really loved it when we could get some girls to go with us. Gotta tell you this one, too. I remember, and I'm confessin' here a little bit if you know what I mean… Robert Earl and I had dates, and we took 'em to the Cactus. Part way through the picture show, Robert Earl and I decided to go to the snack bar and get us some hotdogs, with an extra helping of raw onions to top 'em off. Now, I love licorice. Black licorice is my favorite. So, we got a couple bags of that as well. We go back to the car, scarf down our hotdogs, and start digging into our licorice. Of course, we offer the girls some licorice too, for good measure. Gotta treat 'em right, you see. Then, we thought now is a great time to try a little smoochin' with the ladies, if you know what I mean. Well, let's just say the girls let us know right off that licorice and raw onion breath don't mix too well. No, sir. No kissing,

The Harlem, also known as the "Colored Show"

Doc Bracy's

no nothin'. Shoot, Charlie, we didn't even get a quickie goodnight kiss either. Just can't figure out women, Charlie. Just can't figure them women out."

I tried to keep from laughing as he went on. "You know, we also had our own so-called 'Colored Show' (also known as The Harlem) over on Murphy Street. It was dinky, dirty, and dingy. But, hey, it was cheap... nine cents could get us in!"

"So, you had good times, Mark?" I asked.

"We had our good times, Charlie," Mark answered.

"Okay, what about your favorite places to eat in Odessa?" I asked.

"Well, on our side of town, we kids loved Doc Bracy's. His place was right across the street from Blackshear and, man, we loved his specialty. For about a quarter, we'd get a hotdog bun with half a weenie, piled high with his special chili, and then cheese, onions, and whatever else Doc wanted to throw in there for the day. Now, that was some eatin'. I think he was just priming us kids, giving us young'uns a foretaste of what "Soul Food" was all about! Now, the other place we'd go for lunch was King's Pennywise. Real close by. We'd get a hot link and a soda pop and be set for the day. Another place we liked was Leroy's BBQ. I was friends with Leroy's son, Marvin, and our family had an account set up there where my sister and I could just go over there and get a great BBQ sandwich and charge it. That was really neat, and we loved that."

I thought to myself, *How could one not like BBQ from place named Leroy's?* Then I asked Mark about coming across the tracks and going out to eat places that I was familiar with in the Odessa. "Well, I sure liked Furr's Cafeteria, and Piccadilly's downtown was awful good, too," Mark answered.

"Oh yeah, I loved those too," I said.

"Then there was Johnny's BBQ. Man, they had the best ribs ever! Underwoods was always a favorite, too."

"Yep, I remember Johnny's. Shoot, Mark, me and my buddies would run to Johnny's from Crockett Jr. High at lunchtime just to get one of those big ol' sausage links, where they'd slice it right down the middle and pour on their homemade Johnny's BBQ sauce. With Texas Toast and peppers to boot! Yum, yum! And how about Mexican food, Mark?" I asked.

"Oh, well, everybody knew Manuel's was the best. Those crispy bowl-shaped taco shells, you know, with that spicy meat and cheese right in there. So good I can taste it now!" Mark said.

"I agree! That's where I first had Mexican food. Loved it! And what about hamburger joints and lunch diners downtown?" I asked.

"Oh yeah, there were several along there on Grant Street. Gotta tell you. A couple of those we had to go through the kitchen to get to our table — separated, segregated, and out of view from the White folks in the regular dining area," Mark said.

When Mark was telling me these things, I couldn't help but think how naïve I was... and how sad *this* was. In my ignorance and innocence, I thought these things mostly only occurred in Birmingham, Nashville, Little Rock, Greensboro, and faraway places. Not in the little ol' isolated West Texas town of Odessa.

I asked Mark about this particular upscale specialty restaurant my folks took me to a couple times a year or on special occasions. "Did you ever go to that place over on the other side of town?"

"Well, we tried… sorta," Mark replied.

"What do you mean, 'tried… sorta?'" I asked.

"Well, we went there. But when we tried to go in, we were stopped at the door. The manager told us, 'You can't come in. We don't serve *your kind* here.' But now, you can stay outside, go to the back, and order through the kitchen window and get a takeout. Now, you can do that," Mark explained.

"Oh my, Mark… what'd you do?" I asked.

"We just hung our heads, tucked our tails, and walked to the back and got a carryout… just another sign of the times, Charlie. At least we tried. The food was still good anyway," Mark said.

I suspect it might have been tasty, but I could also sense how there could be a lingering dormant bittersweet aftertaste and feelings of rejection in there… not so much in their mouths, but in their hearts. But Mark moved on from all that stuff. Forgave those folks alright, but still remembered. By this time, I began to feel a little more ashamed and embarrassed of my ignorance as I heard Mark talk. I asked Mark where the family went for grocery shopping.

"Well, most of the time we went right across the tracks to Bishop and Sike's Grocery on Hancock Ave. That was the most convenient. But if we wanted a bigger selection and nicer store, we'd go over to Safeway off W. 8th street," Mark answered.

"You went there, Mark? That's where I used to go with my mother. Just think. We could have passed each other in the aisle some 60 years ago. Been there the same time!" I said.

"Could be! Yeah, I went there with my mom too. That store didn't care what color our skin was. We were pretty much accepted there. One thing I remember getting at Safeway was a nutrition-type milkshake drink called Nutrament. It came in a can, and it was supposed to help you gain weight and make you muscular (360 calories, lots of minerals and vitamins, and 47 grams of sugar). Vanilla flavor was my favorite. I thought, maybe if I drank enough of this stuff, I could get bigger and stronger and play football. It'd help me with the girls," Mark said with a smile.

"Me too, Mark... exactly! I was built just like you. Wanted to get bigger and look stronger. I remember my mom on occasion singing a line from that old 1933 Ben Bernie hit song, *'You gotta be a football hero to get along with a beautiful girl,'* so I wanted to be a football hero. Didn't happen for us, did it Mark?" I said.

"Not a chance, man... not with our little bodies," Mark agreed.

"Right. But hey, Mark, you had that smooth strong bass voice of yours to fall back on. I know the girls liked that. Not for me," I said and continued, this time with a sly grin. "Mark, you know, I couldn't sing worth a lick. I sounded like ol' Barney Fife singing a cappella on the *Andy Griffith Show*. No wonder I was relegated to being page turner for our piano player in the "Sing Song" talent show competition in school," I said.

Mark and I had a good laugh together. Then the conversation turned again to a more serious note. He told me that whenever he was called derogatory racial names (and he was often) he took it upon himself that it was not going to stop him.

"How'd you handle that, Mark?" I asked.

Mark was not going to allow that skewed way of thinking to get in his way. "My daddy taught me to love, not hate. No time for hate. We are to forgive and not harbor resentment. Just move on. So that's what I did," Mark explained.

"You know, Mark, this is so new to me. I just didn't know these things," I said.

Mark continued, "See, Charlie, my parents and my pastor taught me right. There was no room for hate or prejudice in our home or in our hearts... even when we were called names or discriminated against."

What an attitude! I was beginning to love this guy. I shifted subjects just a little bit and asked him what he did for enjoyment nowadays. He said he liked to watch old Westerns and sports (especially football) on TV. He loved taking care of his cat named Princess, but he called her "Miss P." She was a tortoise shell cat and had been his companion for eight years. "Miss P is lots of company and likes watching Westerns on television with me," Mark said. "I think Bonanza is her favorite."

Mark liked to talk to his family on the phone. I was surprised when Mark told me he had 15 kids.

"Mark! Fifteen?" I asked.

"We're all good. We talk pretty often, and I'm friends with all of 'em. I mean, in a lot of ways, I wish it were different. I do have some regrets. Big ones, too. But they know I love them, and they love me," Mark confirmed. "And you know what else, Charlie? I'm just happy with you sittin' right here talking to me, man. You're my friend."

I just sat back and took in those sincere, kind, bonding words. In all my days (and at 70 years plus that amounts to over 25,550 days and counting), I'd never sat in a room having a conversation with a Black man one-on-one before… not like this.

I asked Mark to tell me about his upbringing, his family, and how he developed such a remarkable attitude about life. He told me his grandaddy was smart, went to Wiley College in Marshall, became a doctor, and settled in Sherman, Texas. He said that his daddy, Paul, was smart too and was in medical school studying to be a doctor himself in the 1930's when he contracted tuberculosis. That set his dad back a great deal. He ran out of money, but eventually decided and was able to attend the Gumpton Jones College of Funeral Services in Chicago and become a mortician. After graduating, his daddy moved the family (his mom, younger sister Martha, and Mark) to Odessa in 1949 and set up Prince's Funeral Home Services on the Southside to serve the Black community.

I asked Mark, "What was it like growing up in that kind of environment as a kid?"

"It didn't bother me a bit. Shoot, Charlie. I grew up around dead bodies. I remember as a little fella — three, four, or five years old — just crawling up into an open casket and taking a nap. Good sleepin' in there... soft and cozy. Quiet, too. A little strange, huh?" Mark said with a smile.

"No, Mark... that's a *whole lotta strange*," I said.

We both had a chuckle at that. Mark told me when he was about 15 or so, and on a good day, he'd be able to persuade his daddy to let him borrow the family's green 1958 Studebaker. "Me and Robert Earl and other buddies would tool around the Southside and try to pick up girls. We'd get some masking tape and fashion the words "GIRLS WANTED: INQUIRE INSIDE" on some butcher block paper and stick it on the driver's and passenger's doors. And off we went to see which little lasses would join us in the ride. And Charlie, it worked too! Girls would hop in, and we'd head over to the Blue Front or just drive around the community doing what teens do," Mark said with a big smile.

I thought, *What great memories of being young and free... if even for a few hours.*

"Now, on a really bold day, on Sundays while my daddy was taking an afternoon nap, I would swipe the keys to the funeral home *hearse*, and me and my buddies would sneak off for spin in search of girls who'd like to go for a real ride," Mark shared. "It was a big ol' 1958 black Cadillac with 'Prince's Funeral Home' painted on each side door."

Mark shared with me that even though he was the smallest guy in the group and among his peers, he thought he was really "big stuff" driving around in that big funeral home hearse. Robert Earl and their buddies had no trouble or issues with it, but try as they may, they *never* could lure any of the girls to join them in the hearse.

"One gal told me, 'Mark, I ain't getting there. No, sirree! Only time I'm in that thing, I ain't gonna know about it. Huh uh!'" Mark said with a laugh. "I just couldn't understand it."

"Mark, you should have remembered what our daddies once told us... that old familiar adage that says, 'As hard as you may try, you ain't never gonna figure women out,'" I said.

"That's right," Mark agreed with a grin.

Mark always wanted to play sports (he did run track at Blackshear), but he just wasn't big enough to play with the "big boys" in football or basketball, his favorites. But the Good Lord gave him music instead. He took up piano for 12 years and played tuba for the Kelly Green and Gold Marching Steers Band of Blackshear High. That in itself was quite a feat — especially for a little guy who wore a size 7 1/2 shoe. But more specifically, the biggest talent God gave Mark was his singing voice. A bass voice so smooth, strong, and euphonious that the listener instantly knew his voice was a gift. The girls knew. Maybe Mark was not the all-star athlete he'd like to have been to get the girls, but as he said, "It all worked out okay."

I felt I already knew, but I probed one more time. "Mark, my friend, tell me if you will about your relationship with God."

With no hesitation, he looked me straight on and said, "Charlie, I'm a Christian. Got the Lord in my life... I gotta say, now, you know I ain't perfect. I got regrets. Big-time regrets too. I've done some things I ain't proud of. I strayed from the flock, you understand. But I always came back. Got that forgiveness, if you know what I mean. I love God, Charlie... and you know what that makes me? As a part of God's family, that makes me your *brother*," Mark said.

Then Mark said something that took our relationship to a new level, "Charlie, I love you as my brother."

I had to catch myself for a few seconds. With moistened eyes and the poignancy of the moment penetrating our souls, and without even thinking, those words came right back to Mark from me. "I love you too, Mark."

Then it really hit me. *How I wished all of our divided country today could have shared this moment in time with Mark and me. How I wished those with anger, preju-*

dice, ignorance, bigotry, and bitterness in their hearts toward those of a different hue of skin could experience the sincere, healing words we had just spoken to each other.

It was like a soothing, healing balm had come over us and helped some hard, distant memories become better. We knew that when God, our Creator, is in our midst, there is acceptance and forgiveness, harmony, and love. Mark knew a lot about that. He told me that his daddy once told him that you could take a little Black boy and a little White boy and put them in the backyard and let 'em play and grow up together, free from the curse of prejudice, hostility, and divisiveness of a fallen world, and that those little boys would grow up colorblind. Mark found this to be true so long ago in the sanctuary of the all-inclusive music world of professional entertainers.

So, that's some of Mark's story.

It was quite a bit bigger than I had planned for a newspaper article. Our two hours together that late September 2020 afternoon was a life changer for the both of us. Mark and I grew together as friends, as brothers, and forged a bond that neither one of us could ever have imagined only a few months prior. Only the One who made us both could have planned it.

> *"I know the plans I have for you..."*
> *Jeremiah 29:11, NIV*

Time and Again

By the mid-'60s, The Velvets' recording career had pretty much run its course. When Virgil Johnson accepted a teaching job in his hometown of Lubbock, Texas, that sealed their fate. Mark told me that it was really tough for him because singing and entertaining had always been his true passion. There were a few meager attempts to try to get a group going again, but those fell through, and it would never have been the same anyway. However, the music of The Velvets never died. Those in the music industry, along with fans of the Doo-Wop genre, never forgot just how good and special these guys were.

When Roy Orbison, their friend and early-on mentor, was to be inducted into the Rock and Roll Hall of Fame in 1987, Roy reached out to The Velvets. He wanted them to be there. So, the group went to Cleveland. Clarence Rigsby had been killed in a car accident in 1978 and was replaced by a White guy who was a friend of Virgil's. They were Roy's special guests and sang "Lana" at the ceremony. Roy had co-written that song with Joe Melson back in 1960 and recorded it himself, but it was The Velvets' rendition that he especially liked. It had reached #1 on the charts in Japan in 1961. This event was a very special and memorable time for all the guys, especially since Roy passed away the following year from a heart attack. Glen Campbell, another old friend, was also there. The group was able to hobnob with some of the musicians they'd known in decades past.

In November of 2001, PBS televised one of their nostalgic shows called *Doo Wop 51 Live!* The concert was held in Pittsburg, Pennsylvania. It featured various groups that had helped usher in the Doo-Wop sound. First on stage was none other than The Velvets. As they sang their song "Tonight (Could Be the Night)," all the other featured performers gathered on the stage behind them and joined in on the chorus. (The performance is available to watch on YouTube.) The energy and excitement in the auditorium was palpable. Though The Velvets had another song ready to perform, time ran a little short and they didn't get to sing it.

Their final reunion was in 2010 in Long Island, New York. It was a tribute concert for Roy Orbison. It featured The Velvets (Virgil, Mark, Robert Earl, and two White guys from Lubbock who were, again, friends with Virgil), along with a few other artists. "Lana" was the one song that everyone remembered because of its connection to Roy. For the audience, it was a little different with two of the four Doo-Woppers being White guys — they sang in place of Clarence and Solly — but it didn't seem that unusual for The Velvets. As Mark said, "Musicians don't see color."

Virgil Johnson

Virgil Johnson was born on December 29, 1935, in Cameron, Texas. Early on, he moved with his family to Lubbock, where he graduated from the historically Black Dunbar High School (circa 1953). Virgil developed an interest in music and singing early in his life. He listened to groups such as The Clovers, The Spaniels, and The Flamingos. He joined his church's choir as an adolescent and began honing his own singing style. He sang with a few local groups around Lubbock before going off to Bishop College in East Texas to get his teaching degree. While there, he continued singing with a group of fellow students called The Dynatones.

After graduation, Virgil accepted an offer to teach eighth-grade English at Blackshear Junior/Senior High School in Odessa, Texas. It was there, in late 1959, that four students from Blackshear joined him to form the singing group The Veldaires, which was later renamed The Velvets. The group began performing at talent shows, sock hops, and other local venues. They met Roy Orbison while appearing on a local Saturday afternoon TV show. Roy recommended them to his record producer, Fred Foster, in Nashville. It was a great match, and the group signed a record deal with Monument Records. Over a period of the next three to four years, the group recorded some 30 songs, including their biggest hit, "Tonight (Could Be the Night)," composed by Virgil himself.

The Velvets' recording career ended when Virgil accepted an offer to return to Lubbock and become the principal of Dunbar-Struggs Middle School in 1968. He later went on to work at Alderson Junior High and Estacado High School. He ended his time in academics as principal of his own alma mater, Lubbock Dunbar High School (1985-1993).

Along with working in academia, Virgil also hosted various local oldies radio shows on KSEL and KDAV. He became affectionately known as "VJ the DJ."

Virgil Johnson

In his storied life, Virgil Johnson was a mentor, teacher, administrator, professional singer, radio show host, and family man. Most of all, though, he'd probably want people to remember him as the good Christian and friend he was when he passed away at the age of 77 on February 24, 2013, in Lubbock, Texas.

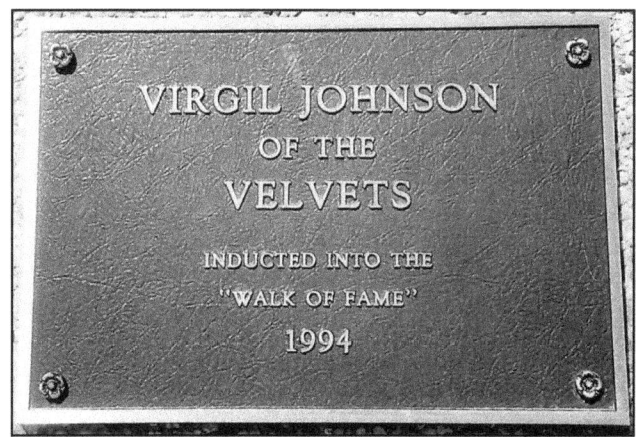

Lubbock, Texas

Mark Prince

Mark was born on September 26, 1942, in Sherman, Texas, to Paul and Lola Prince. His mother, Lola, was of Native American descent. He had one sister, Martha, who is a couple of years younger. The four of them lived in Sherman until 1949, when Mark's dad moved the family to Odessa to establish Prince's Funeral Home on the Southside. Mark and Martha attended Fred Douglas Elementary, Carver Middle School, and Blackshear Junior and Senior High Schools while growing up.

After The Velvets had run its course, and upon graduation from Blackshear, Mark enrolled at Odessa Junior College under President Kennedy's Vocational Education Act of 1963. He became a professional welder. He proudly claimed that he was one of the first Black welders in the region and rarely had to seek work, as the work sought him. He welded pipes and oil field equipment all around the Permian Basin, from Ballinger to Winters and back. He was good at what he did and never lacked for work. Mark married Margaret Anne in 1961 and started a family that included little Mark II, Maria, Perry, Eric, and Marlena. Later on, Mark's years of welding took him to Ft. Worth, where he was employed by American Manufacturing and then General Dynamics, from which he retired.

When he was able, Mark would regularly attend Blackshear High School reunions. At one of those reunions, he received an engraved plaque and was inducted into the Blackshear High School Hall of Fame for his contribution to the Fine Arts. Though the school building itself was repurposed as a magnet elementary, he fondly recalled the people and memories from those years of growing up.

Mark Prince passed away in Fort Worth, Texas on November 11, 2021 at the age of 79 years old.

Mark was inducted into the Blackshear High School Hall of Fame

Welding Training Center at Odessa College where Mark trained

Addendum: Mark's sister Martha became the first ever Black Candy-Striper (volunteer nurses aid) at Odessa Medical Center in 1964. She volunteered there for a couple of years as she pursued her education in nursing at Odessa College. From there, Martha became a Registered Nurse, moved to Ft. Worth, and worked as a Transplant Nurse at Baylor Hospital for 54 years before recently retiring.

Clarence Rigsby

Clarence Rigsby

Mark told me that Clarence grew up in Odessa, right next door to him on the Southside. Clarence had a great tenor singing voice. He was a natural fit with The Velvets and was their "center of joy." The fellows enjoyed teasing him a lot. It seemed like they were always having to wake him up because he had some type of "sleeping sickness."

Clarence was also a great golfer, though opportunities to develop his golfing skills were very limited in Odessa. From time to time, Clarence worked as a caddy at the Odessa Country Club and got to play golf on occasion. Everywhere you saw Clarence, he had a golf club in his hand. Mark said that after the group disbanded, Clarence moved to Lubbock, where he pursued his dream of playing golf. He was so good at playing the game that he once won the Men's Municipal Golf Club Tournament. Shortly thereafter, in 1978, he perished in a car accident.

William "Solly" Solomon

When "Solly" was a little kid, his family moved from Waco to Odessa. Besides singing with The Velvets, he played football for the Blackshear High School Steers. Not much else is known about William "Solly" Solomon, except that folks thought he was just a "wonderful guy." He was the baritone singer for The Velvets, and after the group split up, Solly served in the military during the Vietnam War. He later married a Korean gal and moved to Denver, Colorado, where he worked for a company that made firetrucks. Solly passed away in 2006.

William "Solly" Solomon

Robert Earl Thursby

Born in Odessa, Texas, on December 11, 1941, Robert Earl was musically inclined all his life. "Bobby" played trombone in the school band, had a natural first tenor voice, and was self-taught on the keyboard. He also knew how to read music, and that was quite helpful when The Velvets recorded their music. Mark said that there was never a dull moment in the group because Bobby was quite the talker and always kept them entertained.

Robert Earl Thursby

After The Velvets had run its course, and upon graduation from Blackshear High School, Bobby stayed around Odessa for a couple of years before moving to Hollywood. A short time after that, he came back to Odessa on Christmas Eve, and on Christmas night, he was stepping off a plane in Anchorage, Alaska, where he joined up with his first blues band, the B-29ers. He stayed with them for several years.

He later moved back to Texas, then went on to Denver, Korea, and Japan before eventually settling down in Hawaii in the mid-1980s. It was there that Bobby successfully played clubs with numerous small bands, including his own, Blues Bandits, for years. He and Mark remained close friends and talked regularly on the phone until Mark's passing in November 2021. At the age of 80, Robert Earl is the only surviving member of The Velvets, still writes music, and lives with his wife Delta on the island of Oahu.

Sign of the Times

In many ways, the Black community in Odessa was pretty self-contained. That was just fine with most Odessans. It was when the Black folks came across to the north, east, or west part of town that many of them experienced "issues" that were just a sign of the times — obviously, not just in Odessa, but all across the South, where Jim Crow resided.

Generally speaking, though, the Black community's "well" was a little shallower, a little drier, a little dingier, and a little cheaper than those who lived on the other side of town. The people of color in the area did have their main grocery store in Bishop and Sike's Grocery, which was just across the railroad tracks on South Hancock Avenue. On a bold day, Black Odessans would venture over to Safeway Grocery on West Eighth for a greater variety of food choices, where people of color were pretty much welcomed as patrons. Jay's Foodway was a convenient smaller food store for quicker stops.

The Black community had their own schools (Douglass Elementary, Carver Middle School, and Blackshear Junior and Senior High Schools) and their own football field, which was just a dusty, old, marked-off field with grass burs and aluminum bleachers. They had their own churches and hair salons, along with the Blue Front, where the teens hung out and socialized. They even had their own funeral home, Prince's Funeral Home, run by Mark's dad.

One lady of color, now in her early 70s, told me about an incident she remembered from when she was about eight years old. She was with her grandmother in downtown Odessa. They had finished their errands and got on the bus to ride back to the Southside. She plopped down in the first row of seats right behind the bus driver with her grandmother. They waited for the bus to start moving. And they waited. And they waited. Finally, she asked her grandmother why the bus wasn't moving. The bus driver turned to them and said, "This bus ain't going nowhere till you two take your proper place in the back of the bus." Her grandmother got up and pulled her to the back of the bus. The bus started moving. As a little girl, she just didn't understand. That was 60 years ago, and she still remembers.

She also told me about a time when she and her other grandmother were window shopping on Grant Avenue in downtown Odessa. She spotted a beautiful, colorful dress on display at one of the more upscale clothing stores in town. The dress was so pretty that they just stood there and admired its dazzling design. They knew that there was no way they could afford such an item. In fact, they'd never even been inside this particular store. The prices were too expensive for them, and people of color were strongly discouraged from entering the store.

Her grandmother told her that since she was a pretty good seamstress, if she could find the pattern and do some measuring on the dress itself, she could *make* her one. Around that time, the saleslady from inside the store, who'd been watching them stare at the display, decided to take action. She felt empathy for them and opened the store door to ask about their interest. The grandmother explained the situation. The saleslady looked around to see if anyone was looking, then told the Black woman she thought it would be okay if she wanted to step inside for a moment and take measurements of the dress. The grandmother did so quickly and told the saleslady she appreciated being able to do that. A few weeks later, the granddaughter got her custom-made dress for Christmas.

That was just the way it was back then. Not right. Not fair. Not equitable. Just reality. That being said, there were also many times when White people *were* accepting and affirming of people of color, and were friends with people of color. They gave the Black community the respect they deserved as fellow human beings.

94-year-old Marjorie, a White lady friend of my parents and who recently passed away, told me she had hired help for a few years in the late '60s and early '70s. She needed someone to assist her with housekeeping. A middle-aged Black lady named Bobbie came to Marjorie's house a couple of times a week. The two of them didn't really sit down to talk too much or really get to know one another. However, one time, for some reason Marjorie invited Bobbie, who had arrived a little early for work, to sit at the breakfast table and have a cup of coffee with her before Bobbie got to her chores. Bobbie did, and they just talked. Quite unusual for that to take place in that place and time. It was a surprisingly easy conversation between these two women who both lived in Odessa but in different worlds.

As they talked about family and personal things, Bobbie started to tear up a little, and Marjorie asked her what was wrong. Bobbie told her that her son was graduating from Blackshear High School in a few days, and she didn't have anything nice to wear for the occasion. They sat quietly for a moment or two, and then it hit Marjorie.

Marjorie had the solution. She said, "Bobbie, you and I are about the same size, right? Well, I have a pretty dress I just got and never wore. I want you to wear it for your son's graduation. It'll be perfect. It's still got the tag on it, and it seems like the last time I looked, that tag had 'Bobbie' written on it. It'll look especially pretty with you in it!"

"You would do that for me?" Bobbie asked.

"Certainly. I'd do the same for my sister or friend. And you're my friend, Bobbie."

Both ladies teared up as they took in the moment and hugged one another. Bobbie was one proud, "pretty mama" on that special occasion. The next week, she brought the dress back to Marjorie all dry cleaned and wrinkle free, and she showed deep appreciation and gratitude for that unselfish gesture. Marjorie had reached out of her comfort zone and made a friend with the hired hand.

This is an example of what Mark said to me once: "There's good Black folks and there's good White folks everywhere."

A little over a year ago, through a mutual friend, I was put in touch with a White fellow named Don. He was a few years older than me but had also grown up in Odessa. He now lives outside Oklahoma City. He graduated from Ector High in 1964. Ector High was also on the Southside but was made up of White and Hispanic students only. Black students were not allowed. They had to go to Blackshear even though Ector was just about a mile or two down the road.

Don lived right on the fringe of the White/Hispanic/Black neighborhood, so he had his own perspective. For one thing, he actually saw and heard The Velvets perform at a sock hop at Ector High one special evening. The school had transformed the good-sized library into a dance floor by moving chairs, tables, and books off to the side and out of the way. An area at one end of the room was cleared for The Velvets to perform. Don remembered how fun and unusual it was to have Black people in their school, as Black people were never allowed there. The music was so good, he can still remember them singing the song "Duke of Earl," and that was 60 years ago.

The people of color had a sense of community, but "times were a-changing." It started with federally mandated desegregation and other civil rights legislation pushing out Jim Crow. Things in Odessa did eventually open up for people of color. Restaurants, retail shops, and movie theaters began to accept Black people as equals and worthy patrons. Not quickly enough, but there was progress.

I really do love Odessa. I was and am proud of my hometown. It was a great place to grow up. I had a good education there and have wonderful memories. I have friends who still live there to this day. Located out in West Texas, Odessa was somewhat isolated from some of the bigger problems and issues that the larger cities and metropolitan areas in the country faced in the 1960s. But looking back, I think we Odessans could have done better and ventured out more. We could've been more proactive and reached out to our neighbors across the tracks, just as neighbors should. That's my regret and my loss.

During the time I have left on Earth, my goals are to be more kind, more giving, more respectful, more affirming, and more forgiving to all peoples, especially to those who have been mistreated because they have a different hue of skin than me. In my heart, I know many of these folks experienced prejudice and injustice from those of us with a different hue of skin.

Our country is still not perfect in its ways and attitudes. We have national sins and deep scars that go way back. We need an attitude makeover. I believe it's really not a *skin* issue; it's a *sin* issue. We need a spiritual awakening, a "reset," if you will. With God as our helper, our hearts and minds can be changed. We can change how we treat people who are different than us. We should accept all peoples as God's creations. We should strive to form "a more perfect union," just as it is clearly written in the Preamble to the Constitution of the United States of America. The old spiritual hymn "In Christ There Is No East or West" says it well when the second verse calls for us to do the following: "Join hands, people of the faith, whate're your race may be. All children of the living God are surely kin to me." (John Oxenham, 1913)

Mark Prince lived that life. We need more Blacks, Whites, and Browns like Mark Prince.

Mark Prince:
Just a Regular Guy

As with all of us, Mark had his faults. When reading his story, I think Mark would not want the reader to get the false impression that he felt he was some great, infallible, perfect example of what a person, or even a Christian, should be. Mark had regrets. I think that, especially with his lifestyle and relationships early in life, he wished that he'd done many things differently. With Mark having notoriety at such a young age, he had opportunities and temptations most of us never experience. As a result, Mark fathered 15 children. He told me he tried to do the right thing by them and meet their needs as best he could when they were growing up. He also told me that he had a relationship with them all and talked to them fairly often on the phone. Still, he knew he could and should have been better.

Mark had a conscience, too. The first day I met Mark, we had a two-hour conversation. He sensed my spirituality because I led us in prayer for our dying mutual friend, Pauline. During that "getting to know one another" time, he used some light profanity a couple of times. I thought very little of it, except that he was opening up to me and just being "Mark." The way he expressed himself actually reminded me of my deceased father. On my way home that day, I got a call from Mark. He said he wanted to apologize for saying some of those words. He did not want to offend me.

I told him, "Mark, no apology needed. I'm not offended. Shoot, it ain't like I've never heard those words before. But it just shows that you're human and you ain't perfect. I'm glad you were real with me, man. We're good."

Later, as I was finishing up this book, I asked Mark what he wanted people to know and remember about him. He paused in thought for a moment, then said to me, "I hope that I meant something to people, that I was good at something. You know, that I was a good singer. Now, I had some tough times growing up, but I tried to handle it the Christian way, the only way. I hope people, and especially my family, will remember me as a good person — not perfect, mind you, but one who tried to do good. And that I used my singing voice to bring enjoyment and pleasure to those who heard. And that I loved them all."

That he did.

Short and Sweet Meeting with Mark

One of the last times I saw Mark Prince at his apartment was a Sunday afternoon, late in 2020. From church in Cleburne, my wife, Carolyn, and I drove to Ft. Worth to have lunch with my daughter, Noelle; her husband, Zach; and their little two-year-old, Ollie. Carolyn and I traveled in separate vehicles. She drove her 2017 model Toyota SUV, and I drove my Rangoon red 1965 Ford Mustang. Zach had recently acquired a beautiful dark blue 1967 Mustang himself, so after lunch we all took short spins around the neighborhood in our "Stangs," windows down, listening to oldies on our radios.

I decided to drive over to Mark's place by myself to say a brief hello. I called, he answered, and I told him I was in the area and wanted to show him something. Just a quick stop over, and I wouldn't come inside.

1965 Mustang outside Mark's apartment.

He said, "Well, come on then."

Ten minutes later, I was at his apartment, the Mustang parked sideways right in front of his door. I got out of my car to greet him when he came to the door, looked out, saw my car, and said, "Charlie, what you got there?!"

"A 1965 Ford Mustang. Red on red. And soon, when you're up for it, I want to take you to lunch in it!" I said proudly.

"Well, yes, I'll go!" Mark answered.

"I bet you will!" I said, smiling. "Hey, Mark. I got something else for you. Listen to this!"

I opened the passenger door, ran around the car, got back in the driver's seat, inserted *The Complete Velvets* in the dash's CD player, cued it up to #19, and turned up the volume. It was Mark singing lead vocal on "You Done Me Bad," the *only* song on The Velvets' CD in which Mr. Virgil Johnson is *not* the lead singer.

Mark Prince standing in doorway

"What do you think about that?" I asked Mark.

Mark was so taken back that he could hardly speak. Little could Mark have thought six decades earlier, when he was in RCA's Nashville studio recording that song, he'd be hearing it once again from stereo speakers in a classic car from his era, right outside his apartment in Ft. Worth, Texas.

"Have I done you good today, Mark?" I asked, mimicking the words from the song.

Mark replied, "You done me good, Charlie. You done me good."

With that, I shut the passenger door, hopped back in the car, and turned it around so the driver's side could be closer to Mark, who was still standing in his doorway with his walker, about 20 feet away.

Mark said, "I love you, man."

"I love you too, man," I answered before I drove off.

I thought, *Who could have imagined **this** six weeks earlier? A Black man I just recently met, saying that to me, and me saying it right back to him?* God knows. He arranged it all.

You Done Me Bad

You've done be bad
You've done me bad
You've done me bad
You've done me bad

I never ever dreamed that you would do me like you did me
But it was sad, but, but, but I'm not mad,
I'm just sad, you done me bad.

You were only using me to make him jealous, yessirree.
But I've been had, but, but, but I'm not mad,
I'm just sad, you done me bad.

* **I done you good, I done you good**
I said, I done you good, I done you good.
I gave you all my loving, just like I said I would.
Yeah, yeah, yeah, yeah

Everybody's laughing at me, I was just a temporary fad.
But, but, but I'm not mad,
I'm just sad, you done me bad.

* repeat
Done me bad.
I've done you good.
You've done me bad...

Printed with permission

Where Do We Go from Here?

While writing this story about Mark Prince and The Velvets, I came to realize that these racial issues are so complex and so deeply ingrained in the fabric of our society that it would be much easier for me to just live in the status quo. At the encouragement of family and a few close friends, and after counsel with numerous others (both Black and White), I began delving into books and other materials that address the massively complex, tangled history of the current political and racial divide in our country. What I learned, and am still learning, was sobering, disturbing, and convicting. I've been pondering what I should or could do. After all, I'm just a 72-year-old White guy who writes human-interest stories for my local small-town Texas newspaper.

From my readings and discussions with Pauline, Mark, Tommey, Robert Earl, JoAnne, Tony, Mary, Martha, Ola Mae, Wanda, Chris, and others, I now see how people of color might easily misunderstand the motives and intentions of someone like me — a White, Protestant, evangelical Christian — if I extend an unexpected, unsolicited hand of friendship and fellowship. White folks like to talk the talk, all right, but in far too many cases, we haven't walked the walk. It's been far too little and way too late. Reconciliation is beautiful and is a necessary step forward in order to manifest genuine love, unconditional acceptance, and proper affirmation of the worthiness of all peoples, regardless of skin color or ethnicity. I understand that better now. I've felt the need to go *beyond* and reach out to all people with a soul and heart and spirit, recognizing and acknowledging their worthiness as humans. I'm afraid we White Christians have sat on the sidelines too long without getting in the game.

As a small gesture that I hope leads to reconciliation and more, let it be known that a *Mark Prince Remembrance Scholarship Fund* is in the process of being established at a couple of schools in Texas. It is to be awarded each year to an aspiring first-year music student at the schools. This monetary grant shall start with me: 75 percent of any publishing royalties I receive from this book will be donated there to be given annually to students with talent, character, potential, and need, as determined by the school's music department head.

Other plans to help bridge the racial divide between the people of our great land are also in the works. My great desire is to help people who have been mistreated because of something they can't control. One person, one step at a time. I never experienced discrimination the way Mark did. Never came close. I can't empathize. These issues are too big for me. But not for God. He knows. He's given me Mark's story to help me better understand, so that I might share it with you, the reader. I've written these stories in the book as were told to me by Mark. I've done my best to capture his thoughts and memories on paper.

I met Mark Prince for the first time on September 22, 2020. Since then, I had the privilege of having numerous fairly extensive interviews with him, during which we got to know one another and got to discuss growing up in Odessa. With COVID and health issues, many times we had to resort to phone visits. We laughed and talked some, cried some, and prayed some. Being in the winter season of our lives, I think we both felt that our relationship added a new dimension — a new purpose, if you will — to our existence here on Earth.

In all my times with Mark, we never discussed political leanings. It just never came up. I don't know whether he was a Democrat, Republican, or Independent, or whether he even voted. But in the grand scheme of things, it doesn't matter. When Mark and I get to heaven one day, there will be no superfluous identification labels there for any purpose. Mark and I both believe that knowing Jesus is the only thing that really counts. So, one day, I know that Mark and I will see Him and all His children. This, I love.

My Tribute to Mark Prince

Mark Prince and I only knew each other for 15 months. We started our new acquaintance based on our old hometown of Odessa. I first met Mark at his apartment in Fort Worth in September 2020. We quickly became friends and, a couple hours later, we knew we were more than that... we were *brothers*.

Neither one of us had a male sibling in our families, so in a way, we just adopted each other. We also connected on a spiritual level. Later that day when Mark said, "Charlie, I love you as my brother," I knew this new friendship was going to take me places I had never been before.

All that day, I knew he had health issues. He suffered from severe arthritis, diabetes, blood pressure/circulation problems and kidney disease. So, it was always a day-by-day with Mark whenever I called him. I wasn't sure whether he'd answer, feel up to talking, or welcome a personal visit.

However, when he was having a good day, we did have fun talking about "guy" things such as sports (football especially), favorite foods and restaurants, Odessa's history, regrets, school shenanigans, movies, jobs we had, music, family, recording sessions, and mischievous teenage things. He and I could talk freely about any of those things that brothers would talk about.

Many times, the Good Lord would be a part of our conversation, like how the Lord loves us despite our flaws and readily forgives our sins upon confession. We would talk about how we wished and prayed that our country, and our world would turn to the Good Lord and that all this divisiveness, anger, violence, and hatred would cease to exist.

Mark knew I was writing a book about him, The Velvets, and all these things. I read the first draft of the manuscript to him all the way through to make sure I got it right and wrote what he told me. He was very humbled and loved it. That's how we grew to really love each other.

We had plans, like going to church sometime together... any place he wanted. He loved the idea. I wanted to take him out for lunch and a spin in my red '65 Mustang and play The Velvets music on the CD player for him. He loved that idea, too. My wife and I were hoping to have him over for dinner. But it just didn't happen, as Mark's health really started deteriorating the last few months of his life. He had surgeries, was in and out of the hospital and rehab, and was in a lot of pain.

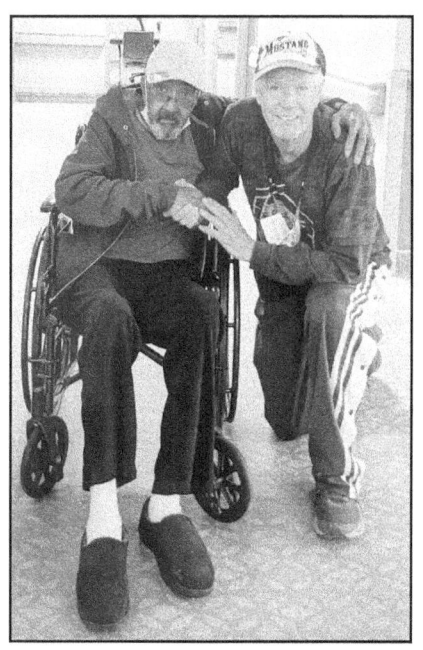

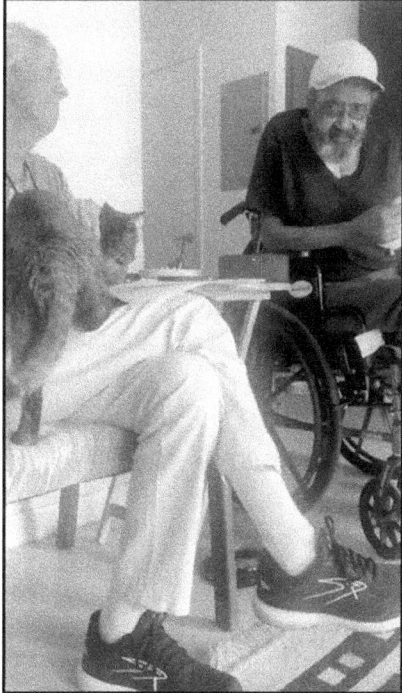

Listening to "Growin' Up Blackshear" with "Miss P" on my lap

The last time I saw Mark, he was alone in his room at the rehab facility in Fort Worth. He was only in a semi-conscious state, but I sensed he knew I was there. I took his hand in mine and told him that he changed my life. With my other hand, I gently stroked his brow a few times and softly told him I would see him again someday and that I loved him. Right then, for some reason, I felt a prompting to lean over and lightly kiss Mark on his forehead. At that very moment, I experienced a release, a holy comfort inside my very being, as I bid my friend and my brother Godspeed.

Mark Prince entered the Gates of Heaven on November 11, 2021. My mother, the *one* person who set my young heart toward the spiritual some six decades ago, also passed away on November 11 in 1995 — 26 years to the day, before Mark's passing. Knowing my mom, I believe there was a little family reunion at Mark's homecoming.

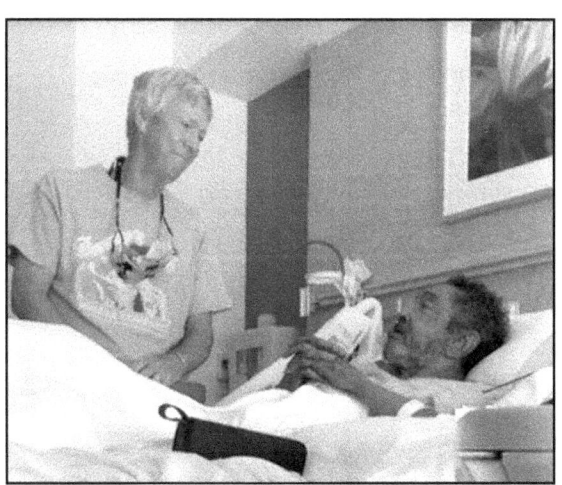

Hospital room — October 2021

...And Beyond

Originally, this chapter of the book you are reading was not planned. But Providential circumstances made it clear to me in May 2022 that the last chapter had not been written yet and would not be until a unique special event in Odessa had occurred the following month in June 2022. So, what you find below is a personal account of what transpired and how this last chapter ...*AND BEYOND* came to be.

In doing early research for the book, I came across a little blurb in the Odessa American newspaper archives (February 1959) about an overflow crowd at Blackshear Auditorium for a local talent show, which featured, among others, The Veldaires (original name of The Velvets). With standing room only and a record crowd in attendance, Mr. Virgil Johnson and the boys (Mark, Clarence, Robert Earl, and "Solly") brought the house down. The atmosphere and excitement for what was happening must have been palpable. How I wished I could have witnessed that happening!

As I continued writing this remarkable story about Mark and The Velvets, the visual image of the group singing on stage to an all-Black audience continued to linger in my mind. For some reason, I also kept picturing Miss Frizella Whitiker (revered high school English teacher for every student who ever graduated from Blackshear, and the matriarch of the Black community) admiring all these students of hers, displaying their singing talents and performing on stage at the school. I suspect Mr. Virgil and the boys could hardly envision where their innate and enormous gifts of singing would soon be taking them — to places they could have only dreamed about months earlier. For me, though, as I continued writing, there was also a fleeting thought that lay dormant for a few months. That thought was the visualization of some type of musical program or event honoring The Velvets out in Odessa. *How could that come about and/or what form would that take?* I wondered.

There were several former Odessa High classmates of mine with whom I had shared in the fall of 2020 Mark Prince's experience of growing up in late '50s and early '60s in Odessa's segregated society. Three of these guys (Steve, John, and Ron in particular) were fascinated with his story and felt a burden of sorts to possibly address some of the issues we didn't realize our Black neighbors across the tracks faced. We conducted a Zoom call in February 2021, and it was obvious we were of like mind and spirit and desired to do *something*. That, in turn, led to our coming together for a brainstorming session a couple months later in Euless, TX. Our purpose was to try to come up with a tangible plan for some kind of event in Odessa... an "endeavor" to do something, something significant and unique, to address some of the tough issues and lingering memories that had been swept under the rug by the city of Odessa six decades earlier. Hardly anyone from Odessa, then and now, had ever heard of this internationally known Doo-Wop singing group, The Velvets, from the Southside. Only those older folks in their 70s and 80s from the Black community had any recollection of their music and legacy. As one might surmise, it was just a sign of the times... not only in Odessa, but other cities across the country, and especially in the South. Out of that meeting, we came up with an idea and a goal to address and change this, as well as somehow bring proper acknowledgement and due recognition to these five lads from Blackshear — and, then, to use The Velvets' harmonious, unifying music as a catalyst to foster new relationships among all citizens of Odessa regardless of hue of skin.

Experiencing and living in the current divisive state of affairs in our great, yet imperfect country, we discussed what we could possibly do to soothe some of these hard memories of long ago and start a healing process in wounded hearts that lay dormant for decades. *Could we initiate some type of Community Unity Event that's never been tried before?* The idea was a little tricky because none of us lived in Odessa, and each of us had gone our separate ways decades ago. But we did have several things in common that forged a formidable bond: 1) We each loved and had fond memories of our old hometown 2) We had respect for each other and one another's various talents and experience 3) We loved Mark's story and how he handled the discrimination and injustices he faced growing up in our fair city 4) We loved the One who made us all and felt He was leading us to do something special and unique in Odessa. Soon, our group expanded outside of our Odessa connections to include numerous other individuals (Gene, Jim, Barry, Steve C., Bob, and George among others) who also believed in our purpose. Along with our core group, they too developed a passion to demonstrate the equal worthiness of all individuals in the sight of God regardless of skin color. Within a few weeks, a couple of us ventured to Odessa to share the story of Mark Prince and The Velvets with those who would listen and to plant a seed of some type of acknowledgement, reconciliation, and affirmation program with number of civic leaders, none of which had ever heard of The Velvets. They seemed intrigued by the possibility of a kind of belated recognition for The Velvets/a ceremony for the city – all tied into the historic, cultural, and musical aspect of the storyline. At this time, things were in the very early formative stages, but the city was open to exploring such an idea with us.

So, approximately 18 months into the thinking, planning, and making, on June 18, 2022, there was a culmination of countless hours of work, discussions, meetings, phone calls, and prayers that evolved into the community-wide event we eventually called, "Remembering The Velvets – Juneteenth

Weekend." This celebration took place in Odessa's refurbished Blackshear High School Auditorium — the very site where The Velvets first practiced their exuberant, infectious music that reverberated across America and beyond. And what a joyous time it was! Some 350 Black, Brown, White (and all those in between) souls joined together to celebrate the music and legacy of The Velvets and the commonality we all share as fellow citizens of this great land. While remembering and acknowledging some tough issues of the past, we focused on how far we've come and what we can all do to make our world a more peaceful, harmonious place in which to live. The mayor, city council, school administrators, various chambers of commerce leaders and foundation officers, local ministers of the Gospel, and common and uncommon folks from Odessa and out of town all gathered together in a demonstration of unity. We gathered in respect and love for one another, which is rarely seen in communities and in the media nowadays. This manifestation of the brotherhood of man made us feel better about one another and about ourselves. Love and tears were all around throughout the hour-long program as we laughed and cried, released and reminisced, while viewing several video clips of the moment that played on the large display screen on stage. We all learned some things about The Velvets and ourselves along the way.

We had the Mayor's proclamation of June 18, 2022 being officially declared "Velvets Day" in Odessa, with a framed certificate being presented to the last surviving member of The Velvets — 80-year-old Robert Earl Thursby from Hawaii. A brief "History of The Velvets" was read to the audience by a Blackshear Alum (the high school was closed in 1966). Dove award-winning musician/songwriter Steve Chapman from Nashville joined

Robert Earl on stage, and the two of them performed two original songs Steve had written especially for the occasion — "Growin' Up Blackshear" and "One Blood." Robert Earl, at one time, left the stage, to greet and introduce 93-year-old Miss Frizella Whitiker in the front row and welcomed her as a special guest of honor in the Auditorium named after her. He gave her a kukui nut lei he'd brought from Hawaii and placed it gently around her neck with a soft, light kiss on the cheek. There was a short video shown on the screen featuring a few of Miss Whitiker's former students and their thoughts on the impact she had made in their lives. Robert Earl then asked Miss Whitiker if she had anything to say. Her answer: "This is such a joy for me. I am overwhelmed. This is such a blessing, and for me to live this long and be able to see the things regarding Blackshear... well, it just thrills my soul. I want to thank anybody and everybody who had a part in this program. It makes me very proud."

Later in the program, Robert Earl sang an original song from his vast repertoire that only added a personal touch to the program and his musical legacy. There was also a Historical Marker dedication on stage for The Velvets by the Black Cultural Council of Odessa and the Heritage of Odessa Foundation, with inscription plaques given to Robert Earl and Mark's sister, Martha. In closing out the program, Robert Earl and Steve's moving duet of the original song "One Blood" reminded us of exactly what we are in the sight of God, our Creator — we're One Blood. And, if we're to have peace and civility in our society and communities around the world, we are to love our neighbor as ourselves. A "Make A New Friend Today" Reception immediately followed the auditorium program and was hosted by the AKA Sorority in the school library just down the hall. Here, attendees could pre-order the book you are now reading. After about 45 minutes of fellowshipping with one another and meeting new people, those desirous of stepping out briefly into the hot Texas summer sun witnessed the official unveiling of The Velvets Historical Marker right outside the front of Blackshear Auditorium.

Enveloped in green velvet and a brilliant gold-colored lanyard (Blackshear colors), Robert Earl and Martha did the honor of unwrapping the covering to the delight and joy of scores of people in attendance... and especially to those who thought this day would never come.

I made a point to seek out Miss Whitiker, as she was about to make her way with her walker to her house across the street. We just hadn't had the chance to talk earlier in the day. But when she saw me, she stopped and beckoned me to come to her. I rested my left hand on her right hand as if we were holding hands. It was such an emotive, surreal moment for me that I could scarce take in the expressive words spoken to me. Others around me heard them, but her words seemed to go straight to my heart — an especially poignant few seconds of time I'll cherish all my days. Her eyes communicated to me what was in her heart. If I could have written weeks and months before what I would have wanted Miss Whitiker to say to me, she said them. What she said touched my very soul and made it all worthwhile. The only thing I can remember saying back to her was, "Thank you, sweet Miss Whitiker. We did this not only for Mark Prince and The Velvets, but for you and the Blackshear Community. And it was a privilege to do just that." This was my calling, our calling... what we're supposed to be about — the constant theme of loving our neighbors as ourselves.

As the crowd began to disperse and Miss Whitiker gingerly made her way with her walker across the street to her modest home, I noticed something that seemed to demonstrate what the afternoon meant to so many of us, and put things in perspective. For those who know West Texas and Odessa, many would likely say that the area doesn't offer much aesthetically to the beholder. It's flat and brown, with few trees, arid and dusty. No real lakes or rivers or mountains nearby to give it much natural beauty. Many outsiders make fun of it, actually. Not me... because of things like what I witnessed with Miss Whitiker after the ceremony. There she was, with an entourage of four to five other people escorting her safely to her home across the street. Two police officers

Miss Frizella Whitiker walking home after the ceremony.

(both White) were there to hold back any traffic that might be passing by (there was none), and a couple of other able-bodied souls surrounding her, with ready assistance should she need it. That's respect. That's being a friend. That's being a good neighbor. That's being the Odessa I know and love.

Well, I thought my story would have ended with that last paragraph. But the next morning I went to church at the invitation of one of the Black ladies who'd been working with me on this Endeavor for the past year and a half. It was a predominately Black church, but she assured me I'd be comfortable and welcome. So, I met her there, and right off I was greeted by two people I already knew and who had been a part of The Velvets' program from the previous day. This was a good start. Another congregant sought me out and told me how much she too had enjoyed the program from the day before. I even got to meet the middle-aged preacher before the service in his office, and he made me feel quite at ease. My friend and I sat towards the middle row of the sanctuary as the music and singing began. The swaying and clapping and shouting in the little choir would definitely wake someone up if there was a tendency to nod off. One lady had a tambourine going so fast and smooth and in rhythm, it was like an extension of her very being. I glanced around this assembly of about 100 worshippers, and I was the only person *not* of color. However, I didn't feel out of place one bit because I sensed I was amongst my "brethren and sistren." I loved the worship because there was no pretense. It was expressive, heartfelt, and genuine. Where there's the presence of the Lord, there is freedom, and I was experiencing that there. The preacher's message was clear and passionate, biblical and practical. I was truly blessed. Toward the end of the service, my lady companion informed me that, in just a couple of minutes, they would be recognizing any visitors, and they'd be expecting me (and any other guest) to say a few words about themselves. Well, I was the only guest. When called upon, I stood up (and obviously stood out), and an assuring peace came over me as I looked around at the sweet Black faces wondering how in the world I got there. The words came easily. Being in the middle of this relatively small sanctuary, I was able to talk to the congregants as if we were friends. I would turn a little bit as I told them, very briefly, about my growing up in Odessa and having rarely ever gone over to the Southside. I told them about how my friend had invited me to join her this blessed Lord's Day in church, and why I was even in Odessa. That segued into an abbreviated tale about Mark and The Velvets and a one-minute version of what happened to me that life-changing September 2020 afternoon in Ft. Worth when I met Mark Prince for the first time. How he'd told me he loved me as his brother. That led into my mentioning The Velvets Endeavor of the previous day over at Blackshear. With that, several people shouted, "I was there!" "Loved it!" "How wonderful!" I had this special, unplanned, unscripted time of connecting, communicating, and communing with my Black brothers and sisters. How sweet it was!

When I sat down, the preacher looked straight at me and said, "Thank you for those kind words. I want you to know you are amongst family here. You said Mark told you he loved you. Well, we love you too. Know that, whenever you come to Odessa, I want you to consider this your church home, because we're blessed by your presence. Please come again. We love you, brother!" Hearty shouts of "Amen!" came forth from the congregation in the midst of his exhortation to me. He had just added to my list of reasons why I still love Odessa.

In closing, I want readers to know that, before Mark Prince passed away in November 2021, I had the opportunity to tell him of this vision of some type of Velvets Endeavor that was in the works for Odessa sometime in the coming year. Of course, he was thrilled with the idea, and he and Robert Earl even discussed it. Though it was still in its early formative stages, he became very excited about its purposes and potential. This future event percolating in our minds gave him much comfort, joy, and hope and took some of his thoughts away from the pain and suffering he was experiencing. So, even as his life was ebbing away, he knew of the planning for a special event to honor him, The Velvets, the Black community, and his Maker. I gave him periodic updates of our progress last fall. He also knew I was planning on donating the majority of any publishing royalties I might receive from the sale of this book to worthy students for music scholarships set up in his name. At one point last October, the month before Mark went to Heaven, he said to me from his hospital bed in Dallas, "We're running with it. We're running with it, Charlie." Though Mark wasn't able to "run with it any longer" nor be there physically for the "Remembering The Velvets – Juneteenth Weekend" celebration program, I think maybe, just maybe, he saw it from the best seat in the house – from on high. We ran with it, Mark, my brother. We ran with it.

"REMEMBERING THE VELVETS" PROGRAM

Host/Facilitator Mari Willis

Author Charlie Norman

Mayor Javier Joven and Councilman Mark Matta with Robert Earl Thursby and copy of the City Proclamation of "The Velvets Day"

"REMEMBERING THE VELVETS" PROGRAM

Sherry Hill of Heritage of Odessa Foundation and Robert Earl Thursby

Steve Chapman and Robert Earl Thursby

Response to "Growin' Up Blackshear"

Miss Whitiker and Robert Earl Thursby

"REMEMBERING THE VELVETS" PROGRAM

Crowd reaction to program

"Make a New Friend" Reception

Sponsored by AKA Sorority

"REMEMBERING THE VELVETS" PROGRAM

Robert Earl Thursby with Martha Prince Wilson

* To view abbreviated video of Velvets Program go to:
Remembering The Velvets — Odessa Chamber of Commerce

CHARLES H. NORMAN III

"Growin' Up Blackshear" lyrics

(Inspired by the memories of Mark Prince)

Growin' up Blackshear
Growin' up Blackshear

Keeping those memories near
Keeping them right here in my heart
No matter where I go
I want everyone to know

About a place I love so dear
Growing up Blackshear
Blue front jukebox
Dancin' in the door

Skatin' rink, Texas dust
Flyin' off the floor
Murphy Street picture show
A dime could get us in

Mighty Steers, green and gold
Still hear that marchin' band
Doc Bracey's hot dog
Half weenie on the bun
Southside, the Flats is where
We'd go to have our fun

We can't forget Miss Whitiker
She loved and taught us all
But oh what dread to hear her say
"I'll meet you in the hall."

We didn't have a lot back then
But one thing we have today
We have each other's love so true
That time can't take away

Growin' up Blackshear
Keeping those memories near
Keeping them right here in my heart

I'm thanking God alone
That I can call it home
This place I love so dear
Gotta say my best years

Was growin' up Blackshear

Steve Chapman/Times & Seasons Music/2021
Printed with permission

To hear/view video montage go to: https://vimeo.com/684389140

"One Blood" lyrics

So many faces from
So many places, yet
Not one looks just like you or me
But what a wonder
When you count the number
The answer will always be

One blood
We are one blood

Flowing heart to heart to heart
It's the same love
We are many colors
But oh how we need each other now
In the eyes of God above

Steve Chapman
*Lyricist, Composer,
Singer, and Author*

We are one blood

We're many nations, and
Congregations

We're city streets and country roads
We're left and right and
We're day and night
We have seven thousand ways to say hello

But we are one blood
And even though we're a million times a million names
Look under the skin, that's when,
You'll see the hope running through our veins

We are one blood

*Steve Chapman/Times & Seasons Music/2021
Printed with permission*

To hear audio of "One Blood" go to: https://steveandanniechapman.bandcamp.com/track/one-blood

About the Author

Charlie Norman has been a writer since his high school days as editor of his school's newspaper in Odessa, Texas from 1967-68. For the last several years, he's been a regular guest community columnist for his hometown newspaper, the *Glen Rose Reporter*. His first book, *Remembrances* (a compilation of 32 anecdotal short stories from his columns), was published by Jan-Carol Publishing in June 2021. His article, "Yeah Yeah Yeah: Music That Moved Us," was published in the national magazine *Good Old Days* in their July-August 2020 issue. Charlie is a 1972 graduate of Texas Tech University (BBA) and earned his graduate degree at The University of Texas at Austin (MA) in 1974. Charlie and his wife, Carolyn, make their home in the country outside of Glen Rose, Texas (named "America's Dream Town" in 2004) and are proud parents of son Charles IV and daughter Noelle. They are especially proud grandparents to five grandsons and one wonderfully spoiled and beautiful granddaughter.

Acknowledgments

Though I've been writing for decades, my experience has been mainly in writing newspaper columns and short stories. But in late September 2020 when I met Mark Prince for the first time, I knew this story, *his story*, merited more than just an article in a newspaper somewhere. In the political, historical, and social climate in which we as a nation find ourselves today, Mark's way of dealing with the prejudice, discrimination, and injustice he faced in our old hometown of Odessa, Texas some 60 years ago should well serve as a template for all of us who desire to live in peace and harmony with our fellow countrymen.

Mark's experiences, upbringing, attitude, and love for his Maker shaped his way of thinking, and it would do our country a world of good to emulate it. Mark was not perfect and readily admitted to his flaws, but that did not keep him from accepting, affirming, acknowledging, forgiving, and loving all people no matter political leanings, socio-economic status, cultural differences, or hue of skin. So, as my first acknowledgment and basis for the book, I thank my friend Mark Prince for his willingness to open up and share his story with me. Little did we both know how close we'd become over the last year and a half. I loved Mark as a brother. He changed my life for good and for the better.

The book itself is dedicated to Pauline Mack, the only person of color I knew in Odessa in 2020 and my dear friend for some 25 years. She was a fellow classmate of Mark's at Blackshear Jr./Sr. High in the late '50s and early '60s and my initial contact on how to locate him. She went to be with the Lord the week I met Mark, but she knew in her spirit that Mark had a story to tell and that "you and Mark will be good for one another." It wasn't until a few weeks later that I began to comprehend what she was saying. I miss you dearly, Sweet Pauline.

Then, there is Janie Jessee, my consultant and publisher with Jan-Carol Publishing (Johnson City, TN). I was just winding up my first book, *Remembrances*, when I called to tell Janie of my encounter with Mark and his story. Right off, she said, "This is special. Every story deserves a book, but *what a story this is*! I will help you."

As I began to share my time with Mark with a few former classmates from back in our days together at Odessa High School, they too grasped the greater significance and encouraged me to write it down. These guys had the same experience I had growing up in our segregated town, divided by the railroad tracks and color of skin — the people of color living on the Southside and the rest of us anywhere else. We classmates (Steve McCleery, Bob Watson, John Carter, Ron Holloman) were a little too young to know much about segregation back then. Maybe we were too naïve, too ignorant, and too caught up in our own world to care. As I shared the stories of Mark with my friends, they each exhorted me to write a book accordingly.

My close friend of 40 years, Steve Chapman, a musician, lyricist, and best-selling author, assisted me greatly in thinking through things from a spiritual perspective and gave me insight into how to better communicate the narrative. I spoke with other close friends from North Texas to Colorado to Tennessee, and they too caught the vision of what the bigger picture was and encouraged me to tell this tale. Through Mark, I've become friends with Wanda Clayton and Tommey Morris — long-time residents of the Black community in Odessa, and they have been invaluable in helping me in my research of the people and history of the Southside. Mark's sister, Martha, has become my friend and readily helped me put some of Mark's stories in context. I've had the privilege of meeting Miss Frizella Whitiker — Mark's English teacher, now 93 years young, and the woman who taught every kid that ever went through Blackshear High School. She, too, exhorted me to write this story.

As I was in the beginning stages of the book, close friends inspired me to keep writing by telling me I was on the right track. Others like Marjorie Marrs, Mary Manitzas, Gem Meacham, Dave and Carla Cheairs, Don Bell, Barry Gregory, Patricia Garcia, and Renee Earls have contributed to the effort in a way only they could, and I thank each of them for their encouragement to me. I'd also like to thank my phone friend from Hawaii, Robert Earl Thursby. At age 80, he is the only surviving member of The Velvets. We've had numerous conversations, laughs, and poignant moments together over the phone and later in person, and I count it a privilege to know him as my friend and brother.

I thank my dear partner and wife, Carolyn, for listening to me (over and over), suggesting certain wordings in my writing and helping me get the manuscript and pictures together for the publisher. She was an invaluable help to me throughout this entire journey, and this project would not have happened without her. I love you and thank you, Sweet Carolyn!

Finally, I must thank my Heavenly Father for the privilege it has been to write this story. Fairly early on, I sensed He'd put me onto something *very special*, much more than just an intriguing human interest article for a newspaper. I knew there was a deeper significance in the message of how Mark Prince handled injustice in our day and time. For those who seek peace and harmony in life and in this world, this book aims to inspire and encourage them. It certainly did me as I wrote it, and it is an honor to share it with you. Our country, imperfect as it is, is still a beacon of hope for freedom-loving people everywhere, and it is people like Mark that give us hope. This is a story of a ROAD TO RECONCILIATION...AND BEYOND.

"Blessed are the peacemakers: for they shall be called the children of God."
Matthew 5:9, KJV

www.ingramcontent.com/pod-product-compliance
Lightning Source LLC
Chambersburg PA
CBHW050815090426

42736CB00021B/3464